Are You Cc

This is to all my sisters who have struggled with
identifying who you really are, through many
tireless nights filled with pain and suffering due to
events of the past, while whispering prayers late in
the night hours, and with everything within, you
decided that your Faith was greater than your fear.

Special Dedication

This Book is dedicated to my father, Mr. Lawrence Harris, who is a Retired Barbour County Educator, and is diagnosed with Alzheimer's Disease. The last chapter of this book was completed on July 25, 2017 on his 70th Birthday. I am honored to be your daughter. I've learned so much from you about life. I love you Daddy!

Acknowledgements

To JESUS…for making all things Possible!!!

To my loving, handsome husband, Michael M. Hardison, who continually encourages and pushes me to greater heights.

To my beautiful, gifted daughters, Jasmine Harris and Bryanna Harris my loves, who support and challenge me and inspire me to move forward into my Destiny.

To my parents, siblings, and granddaughters I love you dearly, and thanks for giving me a reason to grow!

To my beautiful sis, Dr. Cynthia Curtis Steele, who encouraged me to always pray and trust God.

To my beautiful Sister Keeper, Rhonda Thomas who pushed and encouraged me to always think BIG!!!

To my lovely and gifted Sis, Tameka Jackson Hicks for helping design the book cover, and being an awesome writing adjudicator.

To all those who inspired me, prayed for me, and encouraged me along the way, thank you.

ARE YOU CONNECTED 4 REAL?

From Pain to Praise

Katrina Harris Hardison

Contents

INTRODUCTION.............................6

CHAPTER 1:   The Pain.....................9

CHAPTER 2:   The Faith...................18

CHAPTER 3:   The Connection...........27

CHAPTER 4:   The Praise................37

Introduction

Honestly, this year is my year of Breakthrough. I have constantly reminded myself how blessed I am to be walking in the Favor of GOD. Maybe you have had a year like this!!

There were so many times in the prior years that I just wanted to give up. I felt like I was literally drowning in my own blood. I finally came to myself and realized that it wasn't about me, but about the GOD in me.

Previously, I was faced with an inconvenient situation, financially and had to literally start over again. This, however, made me realize where my strength really came from. I had to remain focused for my daughters.

One of the best things I could have ever done was to put all my trust in the Almighty GOD. I have been following Christ for many years and I wasn't going to stop amid my storms. I never took my eyes off my FATHER. Like Peter, I did not want to sink.

I continued to stay focused on my journey by Reading the Word of GOD and staying connected 4

Real!! One thing for sure, I never stopped praying or believing! I knew that my steps were ordered by the Lord. My FAITH was greater than my fear (FAITH>fear).

I wanted to share my story with other women to empower them and let them know that there is still hope after the abuse, the divorce, the pain, etc. You can still stand because you are fearfully and wonderfully made. You were created in the likeness of GOD. You are a daughter of a King.

Maybe you are facing a financial problem, a health challenge, or perhaps a family situation, or maybe this is your Season to be Blessed!!

My Prayer is that this book along with the Word of GOD will help push you forward into all that GOD has for you! Know that you are Destined for Greatness!

Are You Connected 4 Real?
Katrina Harris Hardison

June 14, 2017

ARE YOU CONNECTED 4 REAL?

From Pain to Praise

CHAPTER 1

The Pain

Pain is defined as bodily or mental suffering; penalty. Pain can be dealt with in several ways. Whether it be physical, or mental, it hurts. This means it may injure, wound, or damage you in some form or fashion. When you are truly in pain, you rely on something or someone to remove it.

I must confess…I am not a fan of pain. If I stomp my big toe, I am like a baby wanting a bottle. Let's look at physical pain. Of course, when you go to the physician with a form of pain, He/She prescribes pain medicine to help relieve your discomfort. The pain often leaves for a certain amount of time or sometimes permanently.

I am reminded of "The Woman with the issue of blood" in the book of Mark, Chapter 5. I can imagine that she had a lot of physical pain. The Bible says that she had this issue for twelve years. The Doctors said they couldn't do anything about her physical pain. I began to realize as I began to read the scriptures that GOD provides, so why do we worry about our lives. HE came to her rescue and as she touched him, the issue dried up immediately. Her Faith was greater than her fear. So, all I had to do was allow HIM to dry up my issues. I want to encourage you to stop crying so much, and trust GOD more, just like this Woman with no name. You may be rejected by many, but your life has already been planned by GOD. Jeremiah 29:11.

What kind of prescription do you receive when you are hurting emotionally and mentally? Is there any medication prescribed for the broken-hearted, rejected, abused, etc. If so, do we purchase it or de we just suffer? Good question. Like the Psalmist David, in Psalm 5:1-3. Take your requests to the Heavenly Father as he waits for you to come. This is what I had to tell myself when I was hurting emotionally and mentally from the abuse as a young child. No one knew what I was dealing with. The rejection really made me isolate myself. I was at a point in my life where the pain was extremely cruel and I didn't care about anything. As a result, the betrayal left very deep wounds as a teenager. I allowed others to enter my secret place. I did not know how to get over the PAIN.I began to go into places I should not have gone and do things that were totally unacceptable. I found myself running and hiding from the truth. I probably could have been awarded a GOLD medal for not

caring about myself. This was my way of escape. I was the Queen of fornication at that time. That spirit rested heavily upon me. I thank GOD that somebody was praying for me or I probably would be dead right now. The only sins that most saints see is sexual. By this time, I was a single mother, who according to the saints was the worst sin ever. Baby mama out of wedlock. What about all the other sins I had committed? Sin is sin!! I can relate to the woman in the Bible who had sinned in the Book of John 8:7…When they kept on questioning Jesus about her sin and he tells the accusers that He that is without sin let him cast the first stone at her. How can someone condemn a sinner if they are in sin themselves? In other words, this reminds us to avoid judging others when there are faults in your own life that need to be addressed. We must learn to focus on the assignment, not the attack.

It came to a point in my life where I finally got tired in my late 20's. I was wearing a mask every Sunday. Club on Saturday night, Choir on Sunday morning after just getting in at 5am. Yes, that was me, bet you've probably done the same thing, huh? "It is impossible to be spiritually mature and you are emotionally unhealthy". At the age of 30, I got married for all the wrong reasons, and did not consult GOD about anything. Here I go again, inviting PAIN to come in. Of course, we all know that when decisions are made on our own, it is a set up for failure. After the first year, I wanted out!! I had made a vow (promise) before GOD that I wasn't going to break according to the Word. Learning to control your emotions sometimes means that you do the exact opposite of what you feel. After 10 years of basically being depressed, wearing a mask in church, and fooling myself. Enough was enough and I finally had proof to get out!! I had to go through my painful season THEN to prepare me for my Season of Purpose!!

After all the Pain, GOD still loved me. He still loves you. We may all deal with different forms of pain, but the most important thing to do is allow GOD to heal us. To be healed means to restore, rebuild, and renew. My healing did not have anything to do with an infirmity. It was emotional and mental damage to my mind and soul. One thing that really helped me was that I had to forgive to heal. *Forgive means to stop feeling angry or resentful toward someone for an offense, flaw, or mistake.* Yes, this is the PAIN that really hurts. This isn't a game for sure. We all have an enemy by the name of Satan whose job is to kill, steal, and destroy. He will do anything to keep us distracted and try to stop our purpose. It is your job to let him know that you cannot be stopped. You need to forgive to heal. Are you holding someone in Prison because of your resentment? When we attempt to imprison others with unforgiveness, we are imprisoning and tormenting ourselves. Miracles are unleashed when you choose to forgive. Nothing reveals the health of our relationship with God more than how we respond to those who have wronged us. This will sabotage our future. Anger and bitterness will damage us. In Matthew 18:22 Jesus says we must forgive "seventy times seven" meaning always-no matter how great the offense. Is it hard? Of course, but there is grace available for us. True forgiveness is based on our decisions from the hearts not the actions of others. Well, I know you are asking, how do I forgive someone who molested, raped, abused, tortured, betrayed, and rejected me? Emotional healing is not a result of our own effort, it requires a supernatural work. (Luke 17:4). It is your faith in Jesus and by his grace that will allow you to forgive. It is based both on your decision and the work of God.   Basically, I felt like Hannah (gotta love her) in 1 Samuel 1:13-...Peninnah always picked on her because she had given birth to Elkanah's children and Hannah remained childless. Have you ever been picked on to be picked out? Hannah may have been in pain mentally, but she never lost her faith. She prayed until something happened. To all the Hannah's who are reading this book, do not allow the enemy to win. The PAIN was just as necessary as your purpose. Prayer is the key to being healed for Real! GOD closed Hannah's womb so HE could get

the Glory out of her situation. What is GOD doing in your life to get the Glory? It had to happen!

Healing does not mean that the situation no longer exists. It means that it no longer controls our lives. Tell yourself that your destiny is who you will become. I no longer allowed the damage to control me. At that moment, I was set free. Psalm 77:3 made me realize that complaining only made things worse.

Healing also requires you to be strong. Strong means powerful; earnest; tough, or firm. I had to tell myself that I could handle anything that came my way. Isaiah 54:17 says No weapon formed against us shall prosper. Although so many things formed which caused a lot of PAIN in my life, it did not prosper. You may have some things that have formed a wall of PAIN in your life, but the wall did not stand, meaning, you conquered it. We fall down, but we get up!!

Many people do not bear outward signs of trauma. Yet they have tragedies severe enough to have destroyed them! So glad I don't look like what I've been through. To God be the Glory for being an awesome Healer. Most of us have cracked in some form or fashion. We need to allow the Lord to bless the damaged places of our past. God's arms are available for us to climb and be nurtured. Let the misery go that has challenged your life. In the book

of Job 11:19 the scripture says that we are loosed from those situations that continually haunt us. The inner torment often allows us to hold onto those rattling chains that tie us to our past. Imagine the waters moving in the sea. Allow your past to pass over you as the waters move. Take authority over your situations just like I did. God gathers those who have been rejected. He forever finds treasure in the discorded and confused society. (Malachi 3:17) If a friend or family member has hurt you, they may be hurting. Ask God to heal them, not hurt them. (Miriam and Moses) The Bible says in 1Thessalonians 5:18, In everything give thanks. Can you give thanks when you've been molested, raped, lost a loved one, thrown out of a car, lied on, rejected, talked about, divorced, and a victim of domestic violence? That's a good question. No matter what you are going through be thankful. This too shall pass was my slogan!! Let it be yours too. That's how I was healed. I had been through hell and still gave thanks. Like Apostle Paul in 2 Corinthians 11: 24-28, I wasn't ship wrecked or stoned, but I am qualified to tell you that I am healed from the pain of my past. My FAITH was greater than my FEAR.

One thing for sure, it is impossible to inhale new air until you exhale the old. I began to tell myself that it was time for a "prison break". Just like Paul

and Silas (Acts 16:25-26) I was ready for the chain to fall off. Most of today's adult problems are rooted from childhood experiences. You need surgery. You don't need medicine. You need a miracle.

I was reminded of the Apostle Paul in the Book of 2 Corinthians 12:6-9. He had a thorn in his flesh which had a purpose of torment. Paul was not talking about a literal thorn. Some theorists say that the thorn that Paul was speaking of could have included several things. No one really knows what the Apostle's thorn was but the Bible says it was a source of real pain! Can you relate? Have you dealt with a source of real pain that caused you to cry out to GOD to remove it? The Bible says that GOD allowed the thorn to stay there to humble Paul for HIS own Purpose. Maybe this is why my thorn of Pain remained for so long. I prayed, I cried out, and it remained. No one likes to live in Pain or misery. Paul wanted to be pain free. I wanted to be pain free. You want to be pain free. Know that GOD's power is made perfect in weakness!

When the enemy attacks, GOD reacts. The scripture states in Psalms that, "GOD is close to those that are hurting and the broken-hearted." He knows all about us and our situations. You may not see it, but be assured that He is always working. After the pain, He will bring you out better than you were before.

I was like the Psalmist David...Psalm 119:71. I learned a valuable lesson which caused me to change my life. I did not understand why these things happened to me, but I had sense enough to know that it was all working for my good. It was all necessary! I have benefited a lot through my pains and griefs and I am sure you have too. I became more Godly wise. The abuse, attacks, rejection, and betrayal. It was all necessary. The weapons formed, but they did not

prosper. The Lord washed up my wounds, cleaned up my past, and anointed me for my future. He can do the same for you.

You may think that having to go through pain is terrible. Let's trust GOD. He knows what He is doing. Your pain is pushing you into your purpose!!

CHAPTER 2

The Faith

Faith is defined as trust; belief without proof; promise; and loyalty. According to the Word of God, every believer has been given a measure of faith in order to see the promises of GOD come to pass in your life. (2 Corinthians 4:13) We've all had seasons in our life when the challenges of life seem overwhelming. Your faith is the "not yet", before you get to the NOW. It's what we trust in, but don't see that keeps us going.

I am reminded of the Shunamite woman whose son became ill and all she did was have faith and believe it was well. In my situations, I began to tell myself, it is well. I finally realized that I needed to let go and let GOD!! I decided to go back to school to become a teacher after receiving a business degree and working in the Business field for some years. My thoughts were, "Girl stop fooling yourself. Your dad is a teacher and that is not you." There goes the devil again trying to mess with me! I knew that God's plan was always the best. The process was hard and painful, but I came to the conclusion that GOD was working on me. That's when my faith became greater than my fear. GOD did not give us the spirit of fear. All I did was step out. It is better to move in faith than to sit in doubt. Hebrews 11:1 says, faith is the substance of things hoped for, evidence of things not seen! I couldn't see it at that time; but, I believed it. My faith was crazy and still is. I bet you probably had faith in something you couldn't see either. When you mix your faith with the awesome anointing of GOD, anything is possible.

How was I going to teach with a business degree and no Education courses? Well, there goes that crazy faith. GOD placed me in a position that man thought I wasn't qualified to obtain. By the end of my first year of teaching, my students' data was the same as, if not higher than veteran teachers. My Pastor once said that prayer is the requirement and faith is the anecdote. I trusted God, obeyed him, and let him work in my life. Hence, bring forth the manifestation.

I could not be discouraged by the mistakes of my past. I would not allow them to keep me from my destiny. When we wallow in guilt and shame, that delays us. God turned my mess into a miracle. He wants to do the same for you. Let your faith do it for you. Just like Abraham, stand firm in your faith. Faith moves God and miracles come forth. You can't get to the promise until you go through the wilderness. I realized that my gain would be greater. God was preparing me for my wealthy place. I had to go through the wilderness, so he could humble me. You will go through some hard places in life. It's called living.

Hannah is a powerful example of faithfulness. As you can see, she is one of my favorites from the Bible. Her petition to be blessed with a child was granted after the trial of her faith. She made a covenant with the Lord and stayed committed to it. Hannah's story starts with a distressful cry to the Lord and ends with a song of praise. Her song was prophetic and celebrated God's care of those who remained faithful to Him. We often have no choice when it comes to situations in our lives, but because of our faith we can rest on the promises of God. Hannah is about self-sacrifice done in faith. We must exercise our faith just as Hannah and believe that everything will work for our good. At one point in my life, I felt like Hannah. Our situation was very similar, but my situation turned out to be the complete opposite. I prayed for something to happen and I kept wondering why it did not and at the time I did not understand. Years

later, I got my answer. I just needed to literally, be still. Your waiting is not in vain.

Have you ever wondered why you did not get what you prayed for? Maybe it wasn't a part of God's plan for your life at that time. We all know that God promises that He will be true to His word, but he never puts a timeframe on it. In fact, the Word tells us that we need patience to see the promises come to pass. It takes faith to say, "God I don't know when you're going to do it, but I trust you enough to know that you are able to do it." There is an appointed time that God should fulfill the visions, dreams, and desires of your heart. Just keep the faith. It may take years, don't get frustrated if you feel like you are in a holding pattern. God just may be repositioning things below to ensure a safe landing. That is exactly what happened to me. God is faithful. We serve a faithful God. No matter how impossible things look, know that all things are possible with God. Let your faith increase and walk in authority in the kingdom of God. My husband, Mike, always said his faith was on 1000. At first, I didn't get it because we didn't say that in the south. I finally realized that he meant that it was not wavering. I was like okay country girl, get it together. All throughout the Bible we see people asking for a flood of favor. Elisha prayed that it wouldn't rain, and for three and a half years there was no rain. Joshua prayed for more daylight, and God stopped the sun. Dare to ask and believe God and watch Him move on your behalf. Remember, you cannot stay strong in faith by complaining. Complaining only takes away your strength and energy. You need to learn how to activate your faith in advance. Then you will have the strength you need to wait for the promise.

Your purpose is bigger than you. You may have felt unloved, been abandoned, mistreated, abused, and neglected. Maybe you still are, I don't know, but God does. Imagine the Lord saying, "Don't look back, I know your hurts, disappointments, and betrayals, I saw all the tears. I was right there with you through all the hurt and pain, because you love me and I love you. I will give you a divine exchange, beauty for ashes, but those ashes must be left behind so that I can resurrect those new things in you, daughter." Don't be like Lot's wife and look back. Your destiny is ahead, now walk boldly into your future.

Let me tell you about this crazy faith that I have. This is the kind of faith where you believe it's done, even if you can't see it. My sister in Christ has a single called "Crazy Praise". I believe I played it so much that I wore it completely out. There are a lot of situations in my life where this crazy faith was activated. One situation is, I got divorced after 10 years of marriage. I lost nearly everything that I had. I had one daughter left at home, who was a junior in high school and no job. I had no help with previous joint bills. This included a lovely home with a $1500 mortgage. I had to start all over financially. My house went into foreclosure, my name was in the local newspaper, and on the internet regarding my home. Bill collectors were on my trail. I had nowhere to go. Of course, I did not want to go back to my parents' house, that wasn't happening. I didn't have much time to decide. I prayed and kept the crazy faith, talked to a friend and a door opened for a 3-bedroom house right around the street from my parents' home. I knew that my faith did it for me. It will do the same for you.

You all know the story of Job. The Bible says that He was a perfect upright man. He was a righteous person who encountered such enormous troubles. He insisted that he had no hidden sins and endured in faith…meaning he believed God. At some point in our lives, just like Job, our faith has been tested. If you are facing a test, it is because you are getting ready to be blessed. Tell yourself that you are a VIP in the Kingdom. Pass the test, Job.

I bet you've probably heard that faith moves mountains. Well, mountains do not move unless you speak to them. Try God today by exercising the power of faith with the power of your words, and see him move mountains in your life…and you wonder why the mountain is still there, it's not going to move until you speak to it. I had to stop living in secret sins and be released from bondage. I believe you are ready to be free. It's time to SLAY...I see this all the time on social media. When I say SLAY, don't get it twisted. It has several meanings. I mean knock down some giants like Goliath in the spiritual realm. Every mountain had to fall. I dare you to speak to those mountains and have faith in God. God cannot do more for you than your words will allow him to do. Are you limiting God by speaking words of doubt about a situation? Always speak words of blessings and abundance. Hezekiah had enough faith to turn to the wall and ask the Lord to let him live and not die. He did not keep his mouth closed and the Bible says he was granted 15 more years of life. There is no limit to the power of God. When the Israelites were in the desert headed toward the Promised Land, they had manna to eat each day. After a period of time, they complained to Moses about having nothing to eat, Moses went to God and He said he would give them food for twenty days. Moses thought that was impossible. How could he feed approximately two million people? God said, "Is there any limit to my Power?" All God had to do was shift a few things around and make it happen. God knows how to shift things so the Blessings will fall. The wind shifted and quail fell into their camp. Remember, it's not what it looks like. Activate your faith!!!

I am reminded of the television sitcom <u>Good Times</u>. One of my favorite episodes was when Florida wanted to go back to school to get her G.E.D. and James told her no. One thing for sure, Florida was a woman of faith. Her faith caused God to change James's mind and not only that, he decided to go back to school with his wife. Won't He Do It!!

When there is a travailing in your womb, you can give birth to something new. By faith, you shall live. God will release a level of glory in your life. Just continue to believe that something good will happen to you. Don't remain there. Tell yourself, where you are going is brand new. This place is different than anywhere you've ever been. Keep praying and believing! I had to walk into my new land. My Faith was greater than my fear. (Faith>fear)

Do not be deceived by the tricks of the enemy. The devil wants you to lose your faith and go back to Egypt, that place of torment. Let Egypt stay in Egypt, leave that stuff behind. Tell yourself that you won't go back, can't go back to the place you used to be. The Paralytic man in Mark 2: 3-5 wanted to be healed from those things that had him bound. The abuse, wounds, past, addictions, and pain must leave. He was not going back to that same situation. If you go back, you may die there. He wanted to live. You want to live.

In Mark 5:22-24, Jarius the ruler of the Synagogue believed that Jesus could heal his daughter who was on her death bed. He left her side and trusted Jesus to lay hands on her. He wanted her to live. He had some great faith. Do you have the faith of Jarius? Stand firm and believe God.

You can't put new wine in old wine skin. It would be lost. You are moving forward into your Destiny. Take a leap of faith today!!!

CHAPTER 3

The Connection

Connection means: joined together; unite;
associate

Are you connected 4 Real? Simply means
how healthy is your relationship with the Lord. The
very fact that God loves us is nothing short of
astonishing. We all need a comforter who cares for
us and everything about us. Through all the hurting,
the Holy Spirit who dwells on the inside of us
knows exactly how to provide strength, healing, and
comfort. I found out that it did not matter how big or
small my situation was, God was bigger!! Because
of my connection, the Holy Spirit strengthened me. I
was then able to handle the rejection, mental abuse,
financial difficulties, and health issues. I had to
make up my mind to live my life to the fullest
knowing that victory would belong to me. When
you have a real connection with God, He shows up
like a flood. A flood of favor, a flood of strength, a
flood of blessings, and more. I dare you to catch a
wave of faith and get connected!!! Believing in God
and living for God is different. The question is are
you living a holy life? Of course, the enemy wants
to get you in the wrong place at the wrong time,

doing the wrong things. When we decide to live right, the devil gets upset. It's time to scare the hell out of the devil. Do not allow the enemy to distract you. James 4:7 says, "Submit yourselves, therefore to God, Resist the devil, and he will flee from you." (KJV) When you allow yourself to become soft and weak the devil really attacks. It's time to turn up! As the young generation says, "The devil bout to get his head stomped on!" You got to be that person who wakes up in the morning, looks in the mirror, and cause the devil to say, "UH-OH, Katrina's up!!" I say, "Bring it on baby, you don't want none of this. I am fully armed and dangerous. I am packing in the Spirit. Let me show you what to do with this fresh anointing!!!" You've got to talk to the enemy just like that. I wake, pray, and SLAY!! everyday. "That's what's up", as my husband Mike says with his New York accent. We believe in promises, not curses. We live in expectancy always and never doubt. You should do the same.

Many People today do not realize why they deal with so much unhappiness. Well, it's simple. Just like a robot or a computer, their minds need to be reprogrammed for a real connection. I had to filter the negative input to release positive output on the blessing upon my life. I challenge you today to change your connection. Let your mind be renewed. (Romans 12:2). Start by reading and meditating on the Word of God. This is when a positive connection begins. This will not happen overnight. It is a process. After my divorce, I remember reading, fasting, and praying until it became a habit. This is when my connection really began to transform my life. God wants us to honor Him with our time and stay faithful and focused on Him. I had some distractions during this time and it was very hard, especially when I would see Mr. Tall, Dark and Handsome. I really had to say, "Lord, help me to stay faithful to you. I'm doing good." The devil knows our weaknesses. Trust me, he thought he could get me to mess up, but it did not completely work. I knew that I had been praying for God to send me a husband who loved him first. I did what the Bible said and made my request known. During my waiting, I did not want to disappoint God because of our real connection. It was hard at times, but I knew that the end result would have me soaring like an eagle (Isaiah 40:31). Boy, was I ready to fly!! (Insider)

When you live your life in the Spirit, you have a deeper connection. I often wondered why my husband, Mike would take weeks to study one scripture. It was so much that was deposited in his Spirit. The Holy Spirit leads us daily. He lives in each one of us and teaches and guides us into truth and will bring things back to our remembrance.

teaches and guides us according to God's plan for us.

One thing for sure when you are connected and being led by the Spirit, conviction will come. It's like doing something wrong and getting away with it for a while, then growth comes. You ever went somewhere that you know you shouldn't have gone and something just didn't feel right? The Holy Spirit was telling you that you shouldn't be there. Yes, that's how my life was spared because I obeyed. Learn to recover from your failures and move on in God.

The Bible says that we demonstrate our love for God, by obeying him. Jesus said, "If you obey my commands, you will remain in my love." Listen to God, follow his instructions. Your part is explicit obedience to everything he tells you to do. His part is covering all the consequences that result from your obedience. Obedience keeps our relationship with God open and free. The restrictions he gives us are for our good and help to avoid evil. We have the freedom to walk in front of a speeding car, but we don't need to be hit to realize it would be foolish to do so.

When I first met Mike, I had no idea that the Holy Spirit was leading him to me, but I had been praying for a husband. Us meeting, was totally divine and Holy Spirit led. It was all because of my obedience to the Holy Spirit and a divine connection. After a few conversations, Mike and I somehow ended up hosting "Are you connected 4 Real?" together as a team and the rest is history! The Holy Spirit led him to ask me to be his wife. He did not say, the norm...Will you marry me? He said, "Will you be my wife?" I was like wow... I see you GOD!!! I had no earthly idea that my husband would be from Brooklyn, NY. A couple of months prior to us getting married, I preached a message about the Prayer of Jabez entitled "Enlarge My Coast." That is exactly what God did. My country, Alabama self was connected with a NY City man of God. I did exactly what the Bible said. I told God that I did not want anyone from around here, I wanted him to be about 6'0 bald headed and to love Him (GOD) first. Wow, he came close! He's about 5'11, handsome, bald headed, and really loves God first. The Bible also says, you have not, because you ask not. To all the single ladies, get busy. It will be worth the wait. Now everyone's love story is different, my point is let the Holy Spirit lead you and don't let man stop you. Break free from tradition. Trust the Holy Spirit in you, because he knows what's best for you. Are you connected 4 Real? Go for it!!!

Remember, if you are weighted down with baggage like depression, hurt, pain, envy, financial problems, and abuse. You need to first "release those bags" so that you can be healed before you experience God's full anointing. Allow the Holy Spirit to come into every dark place in your life. Stay in constant communication with God. Release those secret sins and be set free. Get ready to begin a brand-new journey filled with JOY!!!

This year, I hosted a "Release those Bags 2017" Women's Retreat. Through praying and fasting, it was a powerful event. Women were set free, renewed, and refreshed as they allowed the Holy Spirit to lead them. They became transparent and shared testimonies for the first time. These women are connected for real. The best thing we can do is to let go of the hurt and leave the past in the past. You got to unpack some stuff. Our connection will allow us to sow mercy and reap a harvest of peace, joy, and love. Once you realize that you have access to the Kingdom, which includes all that God has for us. You will begin to gain your focus. Access means approaching or entering a place. Spiritually, you can access your freedom, healing, deliverance, and a place of peace. After my divorce in 2013, I was struggling financially, I kept getting unexpected bills which I knew nothing about. The thing that really got me was no one never asked if I needed anything. They all assumed that I was okay. I never let it show, I always kept a smile on my face. I was always independent, so, of course, I wasn't going to ask anyone. It was called pride. There would be times when I would not eat, just to make sure that there was enough to cover all that I had to pay. I made sure that my daughters were covered, even if I had to scrape the bottom of my purses and roll up pennies. No one knows how real the struggle really was, not even my family. My uncle Albert told me before he passed that being too independent was not good, and that if I needed something I should ask for it. This was true. It was my access that helped me get through my financial storm. There goes that crazy faith again. I knew that God would not put more on me than I could bare. I began to pray and rest upon the promises of God. During this time, I became closer to the Lord than ever before. I began to see supernatural manifestation. Bills got paid, money got added to debit cards, unexpected checks in the mail, seeds sown into the lives of my children, and so forth. I used my supernatural key to walk from death to life!! You have access to unfamiliar territory. I dare you to walk through the door of opportunity.

One thing for sure is that GOD always sees the best in us. No matter what your past is, or what you've done, God understands and that's a real connection. People have no understanding of who you are. They try to defeat you. "Hateration" can be used as motivation for elevation. Now I'm going to just let that sit right there. The enemy thinks they are breaking you down. They don't have a clue that God is building you up at the same time. I'm reminded of the time when I was a single parent, with two daughters, the school teacher's daughter! The enemy tried to make me think I was nobody and nobody would want me. I began to tell the enemy, "You are a liar. I will be successful. I will live abundantly, I will get a husband that loves the Lord. I will soar like an eagle!" Because of my connection, I believed that what was in me was greater than anything around me. Your mentality sharpens your reality. The right hook up will allow you to get the right outcome. My Pastor preached a message entitled "I Can Do Bad All by Myself." (Amos 3:1-3) Why are you still hooked up with people who don't have the same direction and destination as yourself? You cannot fulfill your purpose being connected to anybody. Connect with a purpose pusher, someone who will sharpen your iron.

You are anointed to handle anything that comes your way. (1 Samuel 16:12)

Remember, GOD anoints, not man. GOD does not see or judge in the way that humans do. People often look at the outer appearance or qualifications, but

GOD looks at the heart. He evaluates our inner disposition and character. I'm reminded of the blind, lame, lepers, and deaf. They had no place, name, nor value. The lepers had to remain outside the city. Sometimes you may feel like this. I encourage you to not stay there, but go into the camp. I was counted out, the enemy tried to kill me, but I went in. I had to act like I had it long before it manifests. I dare you to go into the camp today. The oil is shaking you. You are anointed for the assignment. You may be an alcoholic, a drug dealer, or a prostitute; it doesn't matter. When the people called you trash, GOD called you his treasure. Before you were born, your destiny was designed by GOD. There is nothing like being able to destroy those yokes.

I had the pleasure of attending a Women's Conference in Enterprise, Al. this year. Christian Girls Rock 2017 really blessed me. I had just returned from my vacation with my husband in New York City. Although I was very tired from the long ride, for some reason, it was in my spirit that I must attend this conference. I called my "Are you connected 4 Real" sisters up and asked if they were going. We decided to go and got blessed beyond measure. I had no idea, but GOD knew. It was a set up. This was my first time attending the conference. Every year the Visionary of Daughters of the King

Nonprofit Organization is led by GOD to crown three women of GOD. I was just sitting there and I heard my name called. I had to make sure I wasn't dreaming. I immediately began to cry and praise GOD for the honor. You will never know the Plans that GOD has for you. (Jeremiah 29:11) I received my crown and thanked GOD for another level. Women, you don't need anyone's permission to be great. This is your life. Straighten up your crown. Queens and know that your COMEBACK will always be stronger than your SETBACK! You got to have that whole purpose, queen ambition, driven go-getter, change the world type of VIBE. Because she competes with no one, no one can compete with her. Are You Connected 4 REAL?

CHAPTER 4

The Praise

Praise is defined as the expression of approval or admiration for someone or something.

I think about David (Psalm 139:14) as he praised God for making him in an amazing way and declared that what God had done was wonderful. Is that how you start your day? Most people put themselves down. David was saying that he was fearfully and wonderfully made. Have you ever been bold like David and said that you are amazing? Don't you realize that God don't make no junk? You are equipped, empowered, and you are amazing.

Make the decision today to stop putting yourself down, your creator says you are a masterpiece. It's time to get into agreement with God and focus on what he says about you. You are fearfully and wonderfully made. Now, give God some PRAISE!!!!

In Luke 13: 10-13, The Bible tells us that Jesus was in the synagogue teaching. There was this woman who was bent over for 18 years and could not stand up straight. Jesus knew exactly what was wrong with the woman. He knew her very weakness. He knows exactly what you are going through. You may be bent over about some situations in your life. The Bible says that Jesus shows compassion for the woman when he calls for her. He is calling for you too. It's time to stand up in praise. I had to unpack some stuff in my life. I became comfortable thinking that abnormal was normal. I was hurting on the inside, and wanted to give up. I began to read the Word of God and a shift began to take place. I just needed a touch and to be healed by the power of God. You may have been hurting because your husband left, you got molested by a relative, you lost your home, or your child ran away. These are all- natural things rooted in spiritual ailments. Only the Master can heal spiritual hurts. The bent over woman stood up in praise. The Bible says and immediately she was made straight and glorified God. Can you think of a situation where He made you straight? Did you give him praise? Today, no matter what you are facing, know that God is greater than all of it. His favor surrounds us like a shield. He is working behind the scenes to fulfill every promise that he has for you.

One thing that I had to realize was that if change was going to come in my life, it was totally up to me. So many people focus on trying to change someone who does not want to change. We must always speak life over our situations and pray for others. There comes a time in your life when you walk away from all the drama, and the people who create it. You surround yourself with people who make you laugh. You forget about the terrible things and focus on the good. You love the people who treat you right and pray for the ones who do not. The conclusion is that life is too short to be anything but happy. Happiness comes when we stop complaining about the problems we have and start thanking God for the problems we don't have. When everything seems to be falling apart in your life, begin to declare boldly that you are resting on the promises of God. We all experience some type of storms in our lives. If you haven't, keep living. I love the quote "Life is not about waiting for the storm to pass, it's about dancing in the rain." That's where the praise comes in. No matter what you are going through, when you depend on God, He will supply all your needs.

We can praise God because He has found favor with us and crowned us with glory and given us dominion over the works of His hands. The grace of God is the favor of God, which causes good things to happen in our lives through faith. Regardless of your circumstances, believe God for supernatural favor which is a gift. I think about

Esther in the Bible, God raised her up out of obscurity to become the queen of the land. He gave her Favor with everyone that she met, including the King. How many of you can say you are not afraid? Regardless of the circumstances, you still believe God.

So many times, in life, we feel like just because we've had a setback that life is over. We need to praise God for our "After This." Those knocks and bruises caused you to rise higher. There will be very painful moments in life that will change your entire world. This is where you become stronger. The anointing comes with the crushing. In 2 Samuel 8:1, David smote the Philistines and subdued them and this is where his victories began. When you go through tough times, the enemy begins to whisper in your ear and tries to make you think you've seen your best days, or you may as well forget about it. It doesn't matter what it looks like. God is your victory. When you are walking with God, nothing in hell can stand in your way. I had to tell myself that after all the hell that I had been through that I knew that something great was coming after all of this. Tell yourself on today that it's not over, this is just the beginning. Give God some praise, and get back in the game. Your setback is a setup for a comeback. You can't fulfill your calling in your comfort zone. There will be haters, doubters, and then there will be you who proves all of them wrong. The woman you are becoming will cost you some friends, family members, and relationships. You are unstoppable!

David said in Psalms 27:13, "I had fainted, unless I had believed to see the goodness of the Lord in the land of the living." (KJV) You are still here today because of God's grace. I had to shift for the better. I had to do things differently this time. I changed my perspective. I had to Shabaq the Lord, praise him like never. You can't start a new chapter in your life unless you stop rereading the last one.

Have you ever been in a dry season in your life? 1 Kings 18:40 the Prophet Elijah asked God to let it rain. During this time Israel was in a dry season. Elijah kept believing it would rain although it didn't happen at that very moment. How many times have you asked God for something and it did not happen at that very moment? Did you keep believing just like Elijah? The Bible says that after about the seventh time around, the servant began to see a cloud arising. There is something about the number seven, it means completion. If it hasn't happened yet, keep believing. Get ready for the rain. Keep going back until something happens. Your greater is coming. The year 2017 is my season of grace and favor. This is the year that my drought is finally over. Everything that I lost is being restored. God will give you more than what you are expecting. Just like the Shunamite woman whose land was restored after seven years, get ready to get your stuff back. God wants to connect you with some true worshippers in this season. We serve an awesome God. He will let it rain on your situation. Tell yourself, the drought is over. Now give God the Praise!!

Are you living in freedom today? You know and believe that God wants to set you free, yet you walk around feeling defeated, rejected, betrayed, hurt, depressed, lonely, and carrying unnecessary stuff. You're picking up junk and it is following you. Oh, what we could be if we stopped carrying the remains of who we were. You don't have to live in bondage when you embrace the freedom that Jesus paid for you. God has a plan for you to be free in every aspect and area of your life. Accept his freedom The Bible says in Acts 16: that Paul and Silas praised God until they were free. He whom the son sets free is free indeed. It was now when I really realized that I was free from all the hurt and pain, that I could now move forward in life. The chains were broken and I could live again. This is your opportunity to be free. Tell yourself that the chains are falling off. Now praise God for your Victory!!!

Do you believe that He will make up for lost time? It's called restoration. (Joel 2:25) Beloved, God knows how to make up for the years you've lost in your life. No, you cannot relive your younger days, but God can make the rest of your life so rewarding and fulfilling that you won't even miss what didn't happen in the past. You may feel like you wasted years in a relationship that didn't work; however, God can bring somebody in your life that's wonderful, attractive, loving, fun, friendly, and tall (My husband Mike), that you don't even remember the years you've lost. Glory!!! You may have spent years working on a job that turned out to be a dead end. You thought you were going to get that promotion, but it never happened and you became bitter. God knows how to make up for your lost time. He knows how to restore. Receive his

promise by faith today. Your best days are ahead of you.

It's not easy starting over, but the best thing to do is to wait on God. I'm reminded of a situation in my life where I wanted something to happen quickly and there was a quickening in my spirit that spoke and said, "It's not time." I was at church in Jamaica, NY and the pastor said, "Do not move until you receive your orders." This was so much confirmation for me. God is telling us to assess our situations and hear from him. Be very careful about your connections. Breed with the right people. Are You Connected 4 Real? God will wipe some stuff out to give you new life! Ask Noah in Genesis Chapter 8. He had to start over.

Let 2018 be your year of new beginnings. Praise God in advance and make Him your focus. This is how you will go from Pain to Praise! Be Blessed!!!

Made in the USA
Columbia, SC
08 February 2025

53041757R00026